I Pledge Alle... to the Flag

D1459873

Stephanie Kuligowski, M.A.T

Consultants

Shelley Scudder
Gifted Education Teacher
Broward County Schools

Caryn Williams, M.S.Ed.
Madison County Schools
Huntsville, AL

Publishing Credits

Dona Herweck Rice, *Editor-in-Chief*
Lee Aucoin, *Creative Director*
Torrey Maloof, *Editor*
Diana Kenney, M.A.Ed., NBCT,
   Associate Education Editor
Marissa Rodriguez, *Designer*
Stephanie Reid, *Photo Editor*
Rachelle Cracchiolo, M.S.Ed., *Publisher*

Image Credits: Cover & p. 1 Superstock;
p. 6, 24 Nancy Carter/North Wind Picture
Archives; p. 7 Nancy Carter/North Wind
Picture Archives; p. 8 Nancy Carter/North
Wind Picture Archives; p. 9 The Granger
Collection; p. 10 Nancy Carter/North Wind
Picture Archives; p. 11 Nancy Carter/North
Wind Picture Archives; p. 15 Corbis; p. 18
The Library of Congress [LC-USZC4-6262];
p. 19 NASA; p. 20 Alamy; p. 20 Getty Images/
Time & Life Pictures Creative; All other
images from Shutterstock.

Teacher Created Materials

5301 Oceanus Drive
Huntington Beach, CA 92649-1030
http://www.tcmpub.com

ISBN 978-1-4333-6968-1
© 2014 Teacher Created Materials, Inc.
Printed in Malaysia
Thumbprints.21250

Table of Contents

American Symbol

Some people call it Old Glory. Others call it the Stars and Stripes. The American flag has many names. It is a **symbol** (SIM-buhl) of our country.

American flag

The First Flag

America's first flag had 13 red and white stripes. It also had 13 white stars.

The American flag is raised long ago.

The stars and stripes on the flag stood for the 13 **colonies** (KOL-uh-neez). Colonies were places in early America.

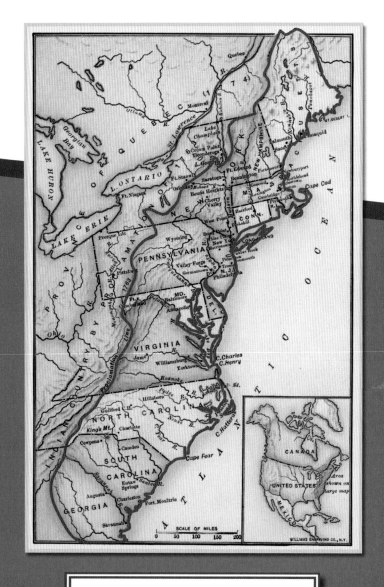

the 13 colonies

Freedom!

The colonies won their **freedom** in a war with Great Britain.

The colonies fight with Great Britain during the war.

The Changing Flag

Later, the colonies became states. The flag changed, too.

This flag has 15 stars.

This flag has 34 stars.

The stars now stand for states. A star is added each time a new state is added.

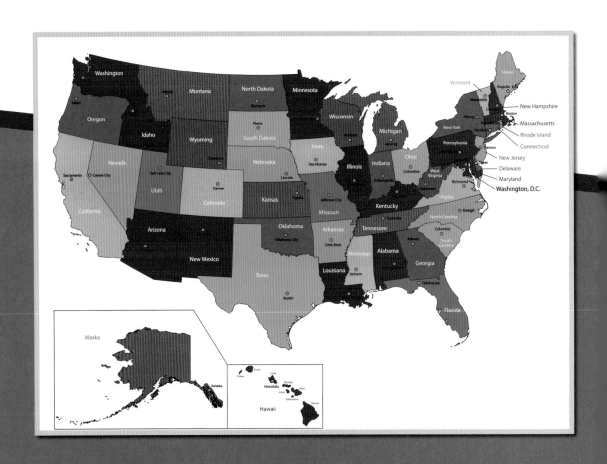

There are 50 states in America.

Today, the flag has 50 stars.

Follow the Code

The Flag Code is a set of **rules**. It tells people how to **respect** (ri-SPEKT) the flag.

This woman and man fold the flag in a special way.

I Pledge

Today, we **honor** the flag by saying the Pledge of Allegiance (uh-LEE-juhns).

These students are saying the Pledge of Allegiance.

Flag Day

Americans honor the flag on Flag Day each year. It is the birthday of the flag.

Save the Date

Flag Day is on June 14.

Flag Day honors this symbol of our country. The flag is a symbol of **pride**. Pride means that we love our country.

Flag Day poster

On the Moon!

Did you know there is an American flag on the moon?

An astronaut shows respect for the flag on the moon.

Say It!

Learn the Pledge of Allegiance on the next page. Say it with your friends. Say it to your family.

Students said the Pledge of Allegiance long ago.

Students say the Pledge of Allegiance today.

The Pledge of Allegiance

I pledge allegiance

to the Flag

of the United States of America,

and to the Republic

for which it stands,

one Nation

under God,

indivisible,

with liberty and justice for all.

Glossary

colonies—places ruled by another country far away

freedom—the power to do what you want to do

honor—to show respect for a person or thing

pride—a feeling that you respect yourself and should be respected by other people

respect—the way you show that someone or something is important

rules—things that tell what you may or may not do

symbol—an object that stands for something else

Index

Your Turn!

A New Flag

Look at the flag above. How would you change it if you were asked to make a new flag? Draw a picture of a new flag to honor America. Write about your flag. Tell a friend about it.